# You Can Conquer
# Life's Conflicts

*by*
*Dennis Burke*

**HARRISON HOUSE**
Tulsa, Oklahoma

3rd Printing
Over 25,000 in Print

*You Can Conquer Life's Conflicts*
ISBN 0-89274-524-X
Copyright © 1988 by Dennis Burke
P.O. Box 150043
Arlington, Texas 76015

Published by Harrison House, Inc.
P. O. Box 35035
Tulsa, Oklahoma 74153

# Contents

1 Letting God Become Mighty in Your Battles   5

2 Focusing on God's Promise   21

3 The Character of a Conqueror   31

4 Faith To Take Charge   37

5 Overcoming a Grasshopper Mentality   51

6 Courage in Conflict   67

7 Victory Upon Victory   81

8 Vision To Possess Your Dreams   95

9 Principles of War   105

References   123

# 1
# Letting God Become Mighty in Your Battles

Throughout the history of God's people, there has been constant conflict. Whether brother against brother — as Cain and Abel — nation against nation, or Adam and Eve against, satan in the Garden. There has been continual conflict between God's righteous kingdom and the evils of Satan's empire. Today a tremendous struggle is going on to bring the Church into a place of truly functioning in God's power. God is rising up in the Church, and Satan is warring against it like never before.

Time after time, when God's people faced an enemy, the mighty God they served would show Himself strong and deliver them. God has always made a way for people who

5

truly wanted to obtain His power for the battles they faced. God is now revealing Himself mighty on behalf of any who will choose to follow Him closely. This powerful, holy nation of redeemed people are coming to recognize that God is their strength and source of total supply.

The Psalmist David came to understand the delivering power of God's might very deeply. He faced many enemies and became one of the most powerful witnesses of that might in human history.

Notice David's insight in Psalm 24:7-10: **Lift up your heads, O ye gates; and be ye lift up, ye everlasting doors; and the King of glory shall come in.**

**Who is this King of glory? The Lord strong and mighty, the Lord mighty in battle.**

**Lift up your heads, O ye gates; even lift them up, ye everlasting doors; and the King of glory shall come in.**

**Who is this King of glory? The Lord of hosts, he is the King of glory.**

"The Lord mighty in battle." Those are such powerful words. They ring on the inside. MIGHTY IN BATTLE. He understands battle. He understands your battles. HE WILL BE MIGHTY IN YOUR BATTLE.

When God goes into battle He will not be defeated. He is the God of victory; He does not know defeat. There is no enemy that can stand against Him. He is the supreme authority and power in the universe.

When you lift your head to see Him and His glory, you become a door for His glory to come in. Through you comes the power to battle against Satan's attack and win on every front. However, many times you may fail to lift your eyes to Him and see just how mighty He can be. You can become so consumed with the magnitude of your enemy's strategy that you forget to lift your head and see either the real source of trouble or the might God is prepared to use on your behalf. Yet, when you look to Him, when you lift your eyes to see Him and acknowledge His willingness to fight for you, He will be mighty and His delivering power will rise up.

Remember this: WHEN YOU MAKE HIS ENEMIES YOUR ENEMIES, HE WILL MAKE HIS VICTORY YOUR VICTORY.

In a war, one of the greatest mistakes that can be made is failure to identify the enemy. Once you see the source of trouble and not merely the symptoms, you can focus your spiritual weapons effectively. God's victorious might will be unleashed to break through any barrier Satan has built.

The word *mighty* used in this psalm implies several thoughts. It means to be a champion, a warrior, a tyrant in battle. God becomes mighty in you as you become mighty in Him. He will crush your enemy and show no mercy.

Of course, when I speak of an enemy, I am not speaking of people. Your spouse is not your enemy. Nor is your employer or the government. You are to love people. Instead, your real enemies are the wicked spirits that have set themselves against God's kingdom, and you are the battlefield.

As the Mighty Warrior goes to battle, you must recognize that His power is as destructive of evil as it is creative of good. Do you remember when Moses stood at the edge of the Red Sea with the mighty Egyptian army approaching to destroy them? Moses had led Israel into a place where there was no escape. Listen to his confident command. **Fear ye not, stand still, and see the salvation of the Lord, which he will shew to you to day; for the Egyptians whom ye have seen to day, ye shall see them again no more for ever.**

**The Lord shall fight for you, and ye shall hold your peace.**
**Exodus 14:13,14**

Moses understood that he did not stand alone at the mercy of his enemy. He was in covenant with the Almighty God. God would deliver them!

Things appeared hopeless. Moses cried to God and God said to him, **Wherefore criest thou unto me? speak unto the children of Israel, that they go forward:**

**But lift thou up thy rod, and stretch out thine hand over the sea, and divide it: and the children of Israel shall go on dry ground through the midst of the sea** (vv. 15,16).

As soon as Moses was obedient, this little nation of vagabonds escaped Egypt by the mighty hand of God. When they arrived on the other side of the Red Sea, they looked back to see their enemies still pursuing them. God's creative power had blazed the trail through the Red Sea — now his destructive force had to be put into operation. You see, it is not only escaping from what once enslaved you, but completely devastating your enemy.

Moses once again had to lift his rod toward the sea, but this time God's power closed the sea, engulfing the army of Pharaoh. The same power that created deliverance for Israel brought destruction to Egypt. Unquestionably, God was ready to free Israel from the threat of Egypt's army, yet it was not automatic. Moses had to act.

In the same way, God wants you completely in control over every onslaught of your enemy. And He is prepared to stop Satan in his tracks. But YOU must act.

If you make peace with your enemy you will never defeat him. Throughout Israel's history, as long as God's people were content to coexist with those who hated God and would not serve Him, they remained susceptible to attack. Whenever they went into battle at God's command, if they did not totally consume their enemy they eventually found themselves under them.

The beginning chapters of the book of Judges tell of some of the darkest times in Israel's relationship with God. After the mighty conquests under Joshua's leadership, Israel failed to maintain a close walk with God. In fact, over the next two hundred years they remained in a cycle of sinning — suffering — supplication — salvation.

They would begin to follow the gods of the people that surrounded them, thus sinning against God. Their sin would always bring them hardship and suffering. When they would cry out to God for deliverance from their oppressor, God in His faithfulness would send them His salvation.

Today many Christians find themselves in that same cycle. They would love to live in the continual victory God has promised. But rather than totally consuming their enemy, they become accustomed to the weaknesses that hinder them — making peace with their enemy. Before long, they are struggling with the sin they have already been freed from. Their lives are simply a series of frustrations interspersed with seasons of calm. They live with little hope of really contributing to others. They are busy simply trying to survive.

God did not call us to survive. He has called us to succeed! He has not called us just to cope with the problems of life. He has made us to conquer the enemies that we face!

In Judges chapter 6 Israel again found themselves in the suffering cycle. They were slowly being destroyed by the Midianites, who had driven them to the point of dwelling in caves. Israel would sow their seed for food. But just as the time of harvest would come, so would the Midianites, destroying the crop before it could be harvested.

God's people had come into the land as a powerful nation that none could withstand. Now they cowered in terror and hid in caves. What a pitiful sight.

Huddled by a winepress was Gideon, a young man trying to beat out a little wheat for his family. There he heard from heaven. An angel appeared to him saying, **The Lord is with thee,**

**thou mighty man of valor** (v. 12). Those words began the most exciting adventure Gideon could have imagined. God was not looking for a man with great natural ability. God needed a man who was willing to take Him at His Word and follow His instructions. Gideon was that kind of man.

Although Gideon considered himself weak, God demonstrated His confidence in him. He called him a "mighty man of valor." What God saw was very different from what others may have seen.

Likewise, God sees you differently than others do. He even sees you differently than you see yourself. But what is important is that you know *you can* be a person, like Gideon, that is mighty in valor.

Strength, power, force, and wealth are all implied in the word *valor*. God sees you clothed with His strength, power, force, and wealth. Before you recognize His might flowing in you, He already sees *you* flowing in Him. You have been made in Christ to walk in dimensions of His greatness which no spirit of darkness can withstand. It is now time to hear the call of the Spirit and allow the King of glory to flow in you with all His might.

God called 300 others to stand with Gideon to see God's delivering power. God gave Gideon the plan that would free Israel from the grip of the Midianites. Vastly outnumbered, the 300 led by Gideon went forth in God's might. God fought for them and delivered them from Midian.

God will move with those who move with Him. Even against impossible odds, if you go in His strength you will defeat Satan's strongholds.

Hebrews 11:32-34 gives some of the most faith-stirring words you can read. "And what more shall I say? For time will fail me if I tell of Gideon, Barak, Samson, Jephthah, of David and Samuel and the prophets, who by faith conquered kingdoms, performed acts of righteousness, obtained promises, shut the mouths of lions, quenched the power of fire, escaped the edge of the sword, from weakness were made strong, became mighty in war, put foreign armies to flight" (NAS).

These people brought God's power into action in the midst of conflict. They met every type of threat with faith in a God who would be mighty in their war. They obtained what was promised. With supernatural power, they combatted any attempt to restrain them or compromise their lives.

That is where you stand. If you are wrestling with weakness, He promises that your weakness can be turned to strength. You can obtain what has seemed unobtainable.

In Daniel 11:32 it says, ". . . but the people who know their God will display strength and take action" (NAS). Because you know Him, you can display the strength He supplies and you can take action.

God is a God of action. His Word reveals the principles that activate His action in us. When you can see how those great people of faith activated God's glory in their lives, you can take the principle and activate His best for you. In His strength you can take action.

The prophet Joel said, **Proclaim ye this among the Gentiles; Prepare war, wake up the mighty men, let all the men of war draw near; let them come up:**

**Beat your plowshares into swords, and your pruning hooks into spears: let the weak say I am strong** (Joel 3:9,10).

The Holy Spirit is calling for mighty men and women to prepare themselves and walk with Him more deeply than ever before. He is calling for us to draw near to Him and to look up. He is calling for us to be mighty, conquering people that will not fall in weakness but rise up and declare, "I am strong."

Your enemy cannot really defeat you; he can only make you quit. If you can see the conflict you face through the eyes of the Holy Spirit, you know the strength to subdue does not come only from your personal ability or willpower, but from the Mighty One within.

Had Israel looked to Jehovah God as they came out of Egypt, they could have avoided years of wandering through the desert. Notice Exodus 13:17: "Now it came about when Pharaoh had let the people go, that God did not lead them by the way of the land of the Philistines, even though it was near; for God said, 'Lest the people change their minds when they see war, and they return to Egypt'" (NAS).

There are those who would rather return to captivity than face a conflict. God has set before you the possibility of living in the realm of the Spirit to successfully wage war against the kingdom of darkness.

You can remain on the sidelines in a place of peaceful stagnation, or you can lift your eyes to see Him as the Mighty One in battle who will defeat every enemy you pursue.

The call of the Spirit is to join His cause to advance His Kingdom and conquer every enemy.

Your battlefield may be your temperament, your marriage, or your finances. God is ready to rise up with you against your enemy. The moment you declare war, His might will stir up in you.

"Finally, be strong in the Lord, and in the strength of His might" (Eph. 6:10 NAS).

# 2

# Focusing
# on God's Promise

On the day when the twelve spies returned from their mission in Canaan, Israel stood on the edge of the wilderness waiting with anticipation to learn their discoveries.

The mighty hand of God had brought Israel from a life of slavery and poverty to independence and wealth. They were free from the ruthless hand of Pharaoh; their commands came only from God. More than 400 years of bitter oppression were over at last. They were on the threshold of great new beginnings.

God had directed Moses to send twelve men into the land of Canaan to search out its goodness. But unbelief prevented ten of them from seeing as God had said. They could see only with the perception carried over from their past days of oppression in Egypt. Their inability to trust God's direction kept them weak.

When Moses sent forth the spies, he charged them to be of good courage. Yet when they returned, their words did not reflect courage at all.

Listen to their report. **The land, through which we have gone to search it, is a land that eateth up the inhabitants thereof; and all the people that we saw in it are men of great stature.**

**And there we saw the giants, the sons of Anak, which come of the giants: and we were in our own sight as grasshoppers, and so we were in their sight.** (Num. 13:32,33).

This did not sound remotely like the land God had described. And the wickedness of their report melted the people's hearts. Their courage and confidence in God disappeared. The ten spies, as well as those they influenced, would never see the promise of God. They would die in a barren land, the plains of Moab, bitter and weary as the result of their own rebellion.

Only two of the twelve men who went to search out the land would ever live there — and then only after their comrades had died. What made these two men different? Why weren't they discouraged? How could they remain confident in the face of the same opposition that terrified the others?

Joshua and Caleb understood something about God that the others never seemed to grasp. Faith in God's Word releases power to destroy any enemy.

Caleb stood before the people and said, **Let us go up at once, and possess it, for we are well able to overcome it** (Num. 13:30).

He knew he was able because he understood where his ability came from. Joshua and Caleb saw themselves strong in God. The others saw themselves as grasshoppers.

Your confidence is largely determined by how you perceive yourself and the things confronting you. On the lips of these two men, you will find no mention of the opposition or difficulties — only words of possibility, promise, and preservation. They refused to yield to the distractions. Their attention remained focused on God and His plan. As Jesus said, **The light of the body is the eye: if therefore thine eye be single, thy whole body shall be full of light.**

**But if thine eye be evil, thy whole body shall be full of darkness** (Matt. 6:22,23).

The thing that you give your attention controls the flow of God's light through your entire being. The reason one person can stand up to adversity and remain strong — while another folds up — is that the eye must be focused on the Mighty One. You can remain in confident rest when you know the power of God's Word is at work.

God said of Caleb, **But my servant Caleb, because he had another spirit with him, and hath followed me fully, him will I bring into the land whereinto he went; and his seed shall possess it** (Num. 14:24).

Caleb had a different spirit. He followed God fully, even when it was unpopular. No doubt he was considered a fanatic. He was different. For forty-five years he stood upon the promise he knew God had for him. He heard the grumbling of the others. Because of their stubbornness, he had to endure the time in the wilderness, yet he never wavered from what he knew. God said he would again stand upon that land of rest and promise.

Let that same spirit of Caleb arise within you. Let the communication of your mouth acknowledge continually the Greater One within you.

The call to all Israel was that they should cease their wandering and murmuring and enter into the life of victory. Their response indicated it was too high and too hard a calling. They would not agree with Caleb when he said, **Let us go up at once, and possess it; for we are well able to overcome it** (Num. 13:30).

It is the carnal person who comes out of Egypt but remains in the wilderness, full of uncertainty. God does not use the wanderer. Notice Hebrews 4:1-3 in the Phillips translation. "Now since the same promise of rest is offered to us today, let us be continually on our guard that none of us even looks like failing to attain it. For we too have had a gospel preached to us, as those men had. Yet the message proclaimed to them did them no good, because they only heard and did not believe as well. It is only as a result of our faith and trust that we experience that rest."

The *rest* that God speaks of is not inactivity. Some have mistaken passivity for rest. Rest is aggressive faith in God's Word to see His will fulfilled — the confidence that He will bring it to pass.

Later in the same chapter, in verses 9-11, he says, "There still exists, therefore, a full and complete rest for the people of God. And he who experiences his rest is resting from his own work as fully as God from his.

"Let us then be eager to know this rest for ourselves, and let us beware that no one misses it through falling into the same kind of unbelief as those we have mentioned."

Rest means to set in motion the spiritual forces of God's Word — not relying on your own cunning to solve situations. Keep your guard up so you do not become complacent and begin to tolerate subtle deviations from what you know to be God's will. Those around you may miss it, but you are eager to know His rest. Others may settle for less, but you remain stable and diligent until you stand in the promised land.

We each have the free will to decide the level of spiritual height we will attain. Some continue in the wilderness of divided loyalties until they die. They become content with only a distant view of their inheritance in Christ. Instead, we must choose to rise up with courage and faith to enter fully into the victory and rest that Jesus has already attained for us. That redemption was too costly, and our liberty too precious to relinquish.

At times the pressure of our present position can look very discouraging. The enemy will launch an attack to beat you down. He will attack your mind with the fear of failure. Jesus warned Peter that Satan would come. He said, **Simon, Simon, behold, Satan hath desired to have you, that he may sift you as wheat** (Luke 22:31). To *sift* means "to break down, to pulverize, or to separate, or to examine closely by testing." Satan wants to pulverize you and separate you from the strength and power of God.

Jesus then said, **But I have prayed for thee, that thy faith fail not** (vs. 32). The only way true faith could possibly fail is by becoming inactive. If your faith remains active, the powers of the enemy cannot pulverize you. Our faith is not in the tangible things we can see, but in the invisible power of the Holy Spirit.

"Since we consider and look not to the things that are seen but to the things that are unseen; for the things that are visible are temporal (brief and fleeting), but the things that are invisible are deathless and everlasting" (2 Cor. 4:18 AMP).

You can rest in God completely when you know His power is activated on your behalf. Look with confidence at the invisible power of His Word and with the anticipation that what He said He will fulfill.

In Isaiah 55:10,11 in *The Living Bible,* God clearly reveals that His Word is self-fulfilling. "As the rain and snow come down from heaven and stay upon the ground to water the earth, and cause the grain to grow and to produce seed for the farmer and bread for the hungry, so also is my Word. I send it out and it always produces fruit. It shall accomplish all I want it to, and prosper everywhere I send it."

The supernatural energy of God's Word focused in your direction will bring down the mountains in your life. It will cause the valleys to rise. It will straighten crooked places and make rough spots smooth. Peace and tranquility will flood your mind with the awareness that all is in His control, as long as you cooperate with Him.

# 3

# The Character
# of a Conqueror

There are leaders in human history who stand head and shoulders above others. They seem almost bigger than life. There are leaders in God's Word who did the impossible through their simple faith and union with Him.

Of the Old Testament leaders, Joshua in particular demonstrated the qualities that are vital to moving forward in God and overcoming every challenge. From his early years of serving Moses to his farewell as leader of this holy nation, Joshua was a man who was mighty in God.

Examining the principles he lived by and the power he possessed can help any believer move from where he is now to where he needs to be in God. Even as a young man facing the unknown hardship of the wilderness, he clearly possessed the simple faith and courage to rise up in God to greatness. The powerful qualities already present in his character would prove to be extremely valuable when he was thrust into the forefront of leadership.

One of these qualities is found in Exodus 24. From Mount Sinai, God called Moses to come up into the mountain to receive the inscribed tablets and the instructions that expressed God's will for this special nation. Moses took young Joshua with him as he went up to meet with God. All others remained below.

Moses ascended alone into the majesty of God's presence, while Joshua waited on the slopes of the holy mount. In unshakable loyalty to God and to Moses, Joshua stayed there forty days and nights. He could have returned to the camp below. But even in a time of feeling forgotten and unimportant, he remained confident in God.

There are times when you may feel out of the mainstream of activity in advancing the kingdom. You may feel alone or forgotten. Can you remain steadfast when there seems to be no manifestation of God's presence?

It is stability and faithfulness that are important. Whether we are experiencing a powerful demonstration of His Spirit or a time of spiritual stillness, we continue without staggering or questioning. We know Him, and we rest quietly in the security of that relationship.

As Moses came down the mountain with the tablets of stone, he could hear a sound coming from the camp. It was the sound of people singing and shouting as they danced in worship to a golden calf. Joshua remarked to Moses, **There is a noise of war in the camp** (Ex. 32:17). Moses dismissed Joshua's observation, certain that it was the sound of singing, not of war.

In this case, however, Joshua's perception and sensitivity were deeper than that of Moses, his elder. There was indeed a war in the camp of Israel. It was a spiritual war designed to destroy God's nation. This same understanding of spiritual battle was the second of Joshua's valuable assets in conquering the land of Canaan.

We must be aware of our enemy's spiritual strategies. Many homes could have been saved and many tragedies avoided if this area had not been overlooked. How often have you seen a simple difference of opinion escalate into a major division in a home? There is a spiritual struggle for the joy, stability, and testimony of that entire household. Rise up with the authority of God's Word and bring the presence of the Holy Spirit into the picture. The climate will change.

In Exodus 33 we see a third facet of the character of this man of faith. After the destruction of the golden calf and the execution of the rebels, Moses again separated himself to meet with God. He had a special tent where he entered to seek the face of God again. The cloudy pillar that accompanied God's presence moved into the tent.

**And the Lord spake unto Moses face to face, as a man speaketh unto his friend. And he turned again into the camp; but his servant Joshua, the son of Nun, a young man, departed not out of the tabernacle (v. 11).**

Notice that Joshua had also separated himself from the people. He preferred to be totally identified with God. This man who had demonstrated his loyalty and devotion to God chose to stay where God would manifest His glory.

Joshua was different from the rest. He was one who stood upon what he believed. He was not swayed by the pressure or opinions of others. He would remain where he would hear the voice of God and then move in accordance with what he heard. What we

35

need today, more than ever, is a renewed dependence upon His Word.

# 4
# Faith To Take Charge

As a young commander, Joshua had followed in the footsteps of Moses. During that time his loyalty to God never wavered. Therefore, God had developed within Joshua important qualities that would make him one of the truly great leaders in Israel's history.

God's first words to him after the death of Moses were significant. He said, . . . **arise, go over this Jordan** (Josh. 1:2).

The time had come for Joshua to move. The mantle of leadership was now on him. He not only had the direction from the Lord, but he also had the courage to act boldly as God's appointed man.

For the past forty years, the Jordan river had separated the Israelites from the land God had promised to them.

Joshua had longed to cross that river. He held fast to his dream of living in the beautiful, fertile land beyond. However, the past forty years had made it clear that before the Israelites could conquer the river and the inhabitants of Canaan, there was a deep need that must be dealt with. They must first overcome the true source of their containment: their unbelief and wrong thinking.

From the day they had walked out of Egypt, carrying the gold and riches of their previous oppressors, the Israelites were a nation destined to be conquerors. God called them out of Egypt into a wilderness apart from any other influence. He brought them into His own personal protection and provision, in order to reveal Himself to Israel.

For us, "wilderness" brings to mind aimless wandering and great adversity. However, that was not the case for Israel in the beginning. Once they had reached the other side of the

Red Sea and had witnessed the annihilation of the Pharaoh's great army, they enjoyed the most marvelous experience in their lifetime. They were free to worship God and know Him. The secluded territory of the wilderness provided the setting for a nation to learn how great their God really was.

God brought them into the wilderness for three reasons. The first was so that they would worship Him. Back in Egypt, God had given Moses these words to speak before the Pharaoh: **The Lord God of the Hebrews hath met with us: and now let us go, we beseech thee, three days' journey into the wilderness, that we may sacrifice to the Lord our God** (Ex. 3:18).

This generation would discover what it meant to be God's own people — not enslaved or bowing down to any other. Until now they had known only the hard taskmasters of the Egyptian empire. God brought them freedom so they could serve Him.

The second reason was that God wanted to reveal to them that He would be their provider. In the wilderness, Israel learned to have confidence in God's provision. It was not easy for this downcast nation to lift their eyes in trust. Though they believed in God's existence, they had never seen Him. How could they expect from Him the essentials to keep them alive? Yet, as a result of their asking, God provided them with fresh manna from heaven and water from a rock.

God demonstrated that He would provide for them even in desert places. How closely we can identify with the struggles these people experienced! In our own lives, the time comes when we press beyond merely believing in God and reach out to discover that He is our provider as well.

There was a third lesson they would learn as they went into this wilderness of freedom. They learned the importance of following God. God provided a cloud by day and a pillar of fire by night to direct their steps. Again and again, they had to pack up and move. God led the children of Israel in this manner. When the cloud began to move, so must His people, even if it seemed inconvenient.

God expects us to follow Him where He leads us. When we yield to His leadership we can stand secure that His plan and promise for us is coming to pass.

Your obedience to follow Him today releases God's hand toward your future. And that obedience is the guarantee that you can obtain that promise.

In the Christian life, it is vital that we get these basic foundations firmly incorporated:

(1) God desires people that will worship Him. John 4:23 says God is seeking after those who will worship Him in spirit and in truth. One of the important foundations of life is that you are created to worship. You are brought

into His presence and lifted as you lift Him up in your worship.

(2) We can look to Him and trust Him to provide our needs. God wants to be God to you. Psalm 37:3 says, **Trust in the Lord, and do good; so shalt thou dwell in the land, and verily thou shalt be fed.**

(3) We must learn to follow His leading and allow Him to direct our steps. . . . **he leadeth me beside the still waters . . . he leadeth me in the paths of righteousness for his name's sake** (Ps. 23:2,3).

Israel's time in the wilderness was not an end in itself. The purpose of this isolation with God was to raise this nation into a new dimension of living. And by doing so they would be fulfilling destiny.

The problems began when they chose to remain in the realm of *provision* instead of pressing on into a land of *promise*. They were reluctant to move from trusting in what had become familiar, into an attitude of total trust in God. They had found a certain security in this desert land where they knew God would provide. He would cover them with His cloud and protect them from the scorching sun. But to move on meant trusting God in the unknown. That is true faith, which they lacked.

Although the call came to leave the land of wandering, they chose to remain in the place of provision rather than going forward into the land of promises. They became so accustomed to the provisions that they would not follow His initiative to press on to the promised land.

We must guard that we too do not remain in a place of mere provision. Of course we rejoice that we have come to the place where we experience God moving in our life. We are grateful and content in Him. But we should never confuse contentment with complacency.

To be content is to be fulfilled. It is to be free from a sense of striving to

be something you are not. In Christ we
have received all things. He has
imparted to us His fullness. John 1:16
says, **and of His fulness have all we
received.**

As the years passed, so did Israel's
generation of faithless leaders. Those
were the men who had brought an evil
report back from the new land, caus-
ing the hearts of the people to melt.
They had spent their remaining years
clinging to the desert of unbelief, until
their bones were buried there forever.

But, thank God, a new generation
had grown up. Seeing the results of
their fathers' disobedience, they had
decided they would no longer be
denied what God said belonged to
them. They were prepared to "arise and
go" with their new leader, Joshua. A
generation of conquerors now began to
control this nation's destiny.

Joshua declared with bold authority, **Prepare you victuals; for within
three days ye shall pass over this
Jordan, to go in to possess the land,**

**which the Lord your God giveth you to possess it** (Josh. 1:11).

Joshua had taken charge! And with this bold stroke of leadership came a response from a people who had come to know their God. **All that thou commandest us we will do, and whithersoever thou sendest us, we will go** (v. 16). The skeptical resistance that once held back this nation was dead. Faith to conquer was alive.

This same faith stirs within you. Faith to live with God's promises as a reality in your life. Faith to overcome those things that have stopped you in the past. FAITH TO TAKE CHARGE! Let the fear and the feelings of inadequacy die. From deep within will spring up the strength to overcome.

Once Joshua began his move across the Jordan river, Israel made a startling discovery. Two men sent to survey Jericho met Rahab, a harlot who lived in the wall surrounding the city. To their amazement, she told them that the entire city was terrified of Israel.

Jericho expected to fall into the hands of the mighty nation that had defeated the powerful armies of Egypt.

Everyone in that region knew the story of Israel's conquest over Egypt forty years before. The inhabitants had waited with dread for the day Israel would cross the river to possess their cities. All of these years, the enemies of God's people had known that they would be overpowered if Israel came in the name of the God Jehovah. Israel was the last to find out!

It is a sad fact that the Christian is the last to find out how complete his victory is in Christ. All of heaven knows! All of hell knows! Satan has dreaded the day that you would see the power of that victory.

Many Christians remain in the dark about their ability in God to overcome the enemy strongholds in their lives. But Satan knows that when God's power is truly unleashed in you, his defeat is at hand. His most successful tactic is to keep you uncertain of God's willingness to move for you. You cannot truly trust one in whom you have little confidence.

All the years Israel wandered in the wilderness, the cities of Canaan feared the day when this nation would come with God's mighty power. Israel finally began to trust God — and the man God had anointed. God now had this nation ready to take the land. They would respond to Him and follow Him in faith.

The Word came now from God, saying, **Sanctify yourselves; for to morrow the Lord will do wonders among you** (Josh. 3:5). This final instruction was needed to complete their preparation. To enable God to do wonders, they had to consecrate themselves.

The same is required of us today. God said the wonders would come. But if they are to come, it will require consecrating ourselves to God. No more holding back, but fully cooperating with Him.

Next, the priests of God, the Levites, were to carry the ark of the covenant, which was the place of God's presence, and stand at the river Jordan. Then they were to dip their feet into the water.

It was the presence of God that divided the waters, but it was the remnant of God's people that carried His presence. Only the tribe of the Levites was allowed to come near the ark.

Today there is a remnant of people that will truly walk with God and in confident obedience carry His presence into any river that lies before them. It is the people of fearless faith that carve the way through circumstances in order to bring freedom to the people God loves.

By their obedience, the priests of God caused the river to stand at attention as the holy nation passed over on dry ground.

**And the priests that bare the ark of the covenant of the Lord stood firm**

**on dry ground in the midst of Jordan, and all the Israelites passed over on dry ground, until all the people were passed clean over Jordan** (Josh. 3:17).

As the nation walked onto the new land, God immediately directed them to take stones from the river and build a memorial. It was to be made with one stone for each of the twelve tribes of the nation.

Victory came because the Levites were willing to carry His presence. However, the victory belonged to the entire nation. Each tribe would have a part of the memorial to God's faithfulness. Their victory would testify to people for generations to come that God fulfills His Word.

Your life testifies to people. Does it testify God's victory? Notice Psalm 92:12,15 from *The Amplified Bible*, "The [uncompromisingly] righteous shall flourish like the palm tree [be long-lived, stately, upright, useful and fruitful]; he shall grow like a cedar in

Lebanon [majestic, stable, durable and incorruptible].

"[They are living memorials] to show that the Lord is upright and faithful to His promises; He is my rock, and there is no unrighteousness in Him."

Your life can be living proof that God is faithful to His promises. You can reflect the greatness of God and His willingness to bring His best to anyone. Everyone wants success in his or her life. People want the results of following God, but not everyone is willing to make the changes that will bring God's success. Joshua was willing!

When the day for action came, Joshua could stand fearlessly because he had allowed God's influence in his life. He had become a decisive man of action.

# 5

# Overcoming
# a Grasshopper Mentality

With the crossing of the Jordan, the days of continual hardship and compromise had finally come to a close for this nation of destiny. There were still many challenges to come. But each would be met with unshakable determination and unwavering faith, rather than the constant complaints and questions of the previous generation.

Under the bold leadership of Joshua, the Israelites saw the fulfillment of the desires they had cherished for nearly a lifetime.

Crossing through the Jordan river and into this new land, they also entered a new dimension in their relationship with God. Their role changed from that of merely following to active cooperation. When they ate

the fruit of the new land, immediately
the manna ceased. (Josh. 5:12.) They
began to move from provision into
promises.

Their destiny to become a nation
of conquerors was about to take on
reality. They were setting their course
to overcome every obstacle that stood
in their way.

As they prepared themselves for
the battles which would face them,
God gave His people a time of rest. It
was a time to renew their strength,
review their plans, and receive new
insights.

It is vital to the progress of any
project to have a clear grasp of God's
direction. Retreating into a time of calm
and communion with Him can be the
greatest tool to prepare you for
progress.

Those sometimes small but
needed corrections in direction are
easily overlooked in the heat of decision making and activity. But when you
pull aside into a time of rest, God will

refocus your attention to those neglected areas.

During their journey in the wilderness, Israel had neglected the covenant of circumcision. Their position of strength in possessing Canaan would depend on restoring their broken covenant.

God had spoken to Abraham many generations before and established this covenant between Him and His nation. Israel must not face these enemies without the confidence that all is well between them and Jehovah God. At Gilgal the nation returned to their covenant and refreshing came.

So many today turn away from their commitment to God, only to find themselves wandering in uncertainty or discouragement. Soon they become discouraged with God's Word. They find it difficult to fellowship with Him or to pray. And rather than remaining in a place where help can come, they pull away, feeling very justified. However, when we learn to remain consistent in our relationship with our Heavenly Father, we will discover a new dimension of intimacy and confidence.

Israel was returning to God with total abandonment. They wanted nothing standing in their way. They had witnessed the weakness of their fathers and now wanted only God's plan for themselves. There comes the time when we must forsake the things that have held us and put ourselves totally in God's hand.

Something happened once their covenant relationship was restored with Jehovah God. The nation's experience in Egypt had taken its toll. They had continued to carry the reproach of their captivity. It constantly plagued these people even after forty years of freedom from Egypt. *They still thought like slaves!*

In spite of all their experiences after leaving Egypt, they still would not allow themselves to think like the conquerors they actually were. They had already seen the utter annihilation of Egypt's powerful army. Yet they clung to a slave mentality.

God had brought them into the wilderness of freedom, but with each new challenge they cried out to be back in Egypt, where they did not face the insecurity of the unknown.

Now notice in verse 9 of chapter 5, **And the Lord said unto Joshua, This day have I rolled away the reproach of Egypt from off you. Wherefore the name of the place is called Gilgal unto this day.** Through the powerful leadership of Joshua — and the new generation of fearless followers — the reproach that had dominated their fathers was removed. The site of this important event became known as Gilgal, "the place of removal or rolling."

The stigma of slavery was no longer a part of their thoughts. They had truly entered a new land. But even more important, they had entered a new relationship with God Almighty.

Our attitude toward ourselves holds a significant place in our success and in our achievement in growing in the Kingdom of God. How do we see ourselves? Are we receiving our mental stability from Christ, or are we governed by thoughts of past failures? Can we receive ideas from the Holy Spirit to deal with the issues we face, or are we confining ourselves to carnal answers? The old carnal attitudes and ideas will not bring about the kind of power or results you long to see.

The Apostle Paul mentions the importance of right thinking many times. When you are "renewed in the spirit of your mind" as Ephesians 4:23 directs, you set aside the slavery syndrome and put on a conquering consciousness. You learn that the endless opportunity to become offended and discouraged can be replaced by a commitment to contentment.

By choosing the right thoughts, you lift your own life. You choose the thoughts that are consistent with God's Word. When God has said you are an overcomer, then to think like an overcomer you replace thoughts of defeat and failure with God's Word. Your thoughts are like seeds planted in your own life. Your mind is like a garden. You can cultivate your mind and plant the seeds you want to grow, or you can neglect it and allow weeds to take over. Either way, it will bring a harvest into your life.

Galatians 6:7 declares a most important truth. Notice the Phillips translation, "A man's harvest in life will depend entirely on what he sows."

Israel had known only slavery. The people were programmed to think like slaves, respond like slaves, and act like slaves. God was moving them out of slavery and reprogramming them to be a conquering nation.

The way you perceive challenges is determined by the way you have been programmed. Seeds of slavery can remain in your thoughts and stifle your growth. The Bible says in Proverbs 23:7, **For as he thinketh in his heart, so is he.** The word "heart" in this verse is nearly always translated "soul" in other scriptures. This verse is saying that what a person really thinks deep within himself is what he becomes. Therefore, we must look beyond what is actually said and determine what is within the heart.

We learn that the way to affect our own lives is to modify the way we think. As you begin to regard yourself in a constructive, positive way based upon God's Word, you release spiritual power in your life through your soul.

You see, the realm of the soul is the connecting point between the spiritual realm and the physical realm. The mind, will, and emotions make up the soulish realm.

When you yield your soul to be renewed by *God's* Words and thoughts, you see yourself from an entirely new perspective. You realize that you are what God has made you in Christ. You are righteous because you are in Him and there is no unrighteousness in Him. You are free from past mistakes. You are liberated from your weakness and filled to overflowing with His strength. These are but a few of the beautiful deposits of God's great wealth within you. The more your thoughts are in accord with the deposit God has made, the greater the release into your life.

You can remain a captive of your thoughts, or you can change the way you are by harmonizing your thoughts with God's thoughts. In his powerful book entitled *Seeds of Greatness*, Dr. Denis Waitley writes, "Our mind can't tell the difference between real experience and one that is vividly and repeatedly imagined."*

Understanding the power of your imagination is a key secret to releasing the power of God's Word in your life. When you begin to imagine yourself as

---

* (Old Tappan: Fleming H. Revell, 1983).

though His Words and promises are already working in you, the power of those promises is released and activated within you.

One man told how he had received a diagnosis of terminal cancer. He knew little about God, but when faced with death he began to evaluate his life and his relationship with God.

He reasoned that if God was good, then God certainly wanted him to be healed. That idea became a reality in his mind. As he sat at home, he began to create mental pictures of massive armies of white blood cells gathering forces and then charging through his body to attack the cancer. He envisioned wave after wave of white blood cells surging through his body. Of course, this was all taking place in his mind.

Later, when he went for his treatments his doctors announced with some surprise, "You are in remission." That declaration was made nine years ago at the time of this writing.

God's power is released in us as we cooperate with Him and activate that power. As you think so you are. You are moving toward your most dominant thoughts. Jesus paid a great price for you to live in health; it is a vital part of redemption. If you do not see yourself overcoming disease, you can create new pictures in your mind of His health in your body.

How do you see your family? Choose to see your family as God intends it to be — full of love, kindness, and tenderness toward one another. How do you view your job? Apply God's Word to your thoughts to bring about peace, promotion, or obtaining that new position.

This is more than mental power. When your thoughts harmonize with God's Word, His power can work through you. Using mental pictures from God's Word causes the reality of His promises to lodge deep into your heart. You must plant the seed of His promise and purposely cultivate it exactly the way a farmer would. That seed will produce a bountiful harvest as you willfully nurture it.

Israel had been defeated for forty years by the enemy of their own imagination. They were like grasshoppers in their *own sight*. Their halfhearted service to God had limited them. Israel could escape from Egypt but not this wilderness. They were under a reproach. However, there was a new generation ready to respond to any direction God might give. They were no longer a nation of wandering vagabonds in the desert, but a people determined to take the land that belonged to them. Their thoughts were finally in harmony with God.

As Joshua considered his course of action and wondered how his untrained men could take such a formidable fortress as Jericho, suddenly he saw before him the Prince of the Host of Jehovah. Joshua fell on his face in His mighty presence and at the direction of the Prince, he removed his shoes from his feet, for he was on holy ground.

Joshua remembered how Moses had told of the fearful, yet beautiful experience of hearing God's voice from the burning bush and himself standing on holy ground. Now, in the footsteps of his predecessor, Joshua would experience the same unforgettable presence.

The Prince assured Joshua of victory over Jericho before giving him the detailed plan. "Jericho and its king and all its mighty warriors are already defeated, for I have given them to you" (Josh. 6:2 TLB).

Notice how God focused first on the end result. Then He instructed Joshua on how to obtain that victory. They were to go repeatedly around the wall of Jericho, led by the Ark of the Lord.

Many times we confuse this simple but important order of progression. If we have the wrong end result in mind, we will only misunderstand the details. On the other hand, if we do see the end results but never press in to discover the details or the plan, we will remain with only the hope of God's promise but not the reality.

Joshua knew that not only was Jericho's overthrow divinely commissioned, but also that God was empowering the Israelites with His wisdom and strength.

Israel stood and looked at a city that appeared to be impenetrable. But Israel had come in the name of the Lord their God. The great walls of the city could restrain them no longer.

To the last detail, the Israelites followed the instructions they had received. Thirteen times they compassed the city, without speaking. The only sound was the reverberation of the priest's trumpets made from rams' horns. The same trumpets were sounded every fifty years to declare the year of Jubilee. Now, they announced the presence of a conquering God and His mighty people. After the seventh time on the seventh day of marching, the priests blew the trumpets again. This time, the people shouted as loudly as they could. Because they had obeyed God's plan, the walls of Jericho fell flat at their feet. The city was taken. Israel was vindicated, and they experienced the promise God had made to them.

There may be walls that have restrained you. There may be barriers of wrong thinking that prevent you from experiencing the goodness God has freely given. But at the shout of God's Word from your lips, thoughts of negativism and strife, thoughts of failure, or thoughts of lack will begin to crumble.

Jesus has announced your deliverance. The trumpet of Jubilee has sounded. Now let the shout of victory be declared!

# 6

# Courage in Conflict

The success at Jericho demonstrated clearly that Joshua had taken position as the commander of Israel with an astonishing sense of leadership. There was no question that he was fearlessly following Jehovah's command.

One of the key ingredients of his sweeping success was his courage to carry out even the most peculiar strategies. Courage enabled Joshua to see from God's perspective and know how to receive what God had promised Moses. God had said to him, **Only be thou strong and very courageous, that thou mayest observe to do according to all the law, which Moses my servant commanded thee** (Josh. 1:7).

The only way you can accurately determine the direction God is leading you is to see a situation from a perspective of His strength and courage. Trying to perceive God's direction through the eyes of your own weakness will always leave you frustrated. Even your own strength and willpower cannot put you over. It is God's courage in conflict that brings conquest.

Courage is firmness in the face of danger or difficulty. The dictionary shows that our English word "courage" is derived from the French word "cuer" or heart.* It means to have the heart as the seat of intelligence. To be courageous is to be led by your heart, not merely your reasoning — putting your thoughts and imaginations under the control of Holy Spirit-inspired ideas.

It truly takes courage to follow God rather than the path of least resistance. It can mean making a decision, or taking a stand that is unpopular and may generate criticism.

---

* *Webster's New Collegiate Dictionary*, S. V. "Courage."

But most important is loyalty to God, even when it costs the adulation of people.

Both Joshua and Caleb took a very lonely stand when they first returned from the land of promise with a report of victory. They were rejected and ignored. Yet they stood courageously upon the promise God had made to them. They would not be distracted, but rather they remained loyal to what they knew deep in their hearts to be true. Their minds remained steadfast and established — they would not be swayed.

Years later, this same courage stirred through Joshua as he approached the city of Jericho. It took leadership beyond the limits of accepted strategies to entertain the concept of God's plan that brought that city down.

He had to follow his heart, not his mind. The plan God made alive within him was to be followed even though it was not reasonable. Every conquest was not as dramatic as Jericho, but the assurance of victory was always there. When God said to go and conquer, they knew the result would be victory. It is this same courage that will enable you to win over the weaknesses and the challenges that face you.

Courage can always be understood as having a "buoyant spirit" — the kind of attitude that just will not be put down or made bitter because of the bumps of life or the attacks of the enemy. A buoyant spirit always comes back up. Hard times and difficulties attempt to discourage you, to drain you of courage, but having a buoyant spirit you always come up. There can be a spring within you that always thrusts you up above the trouble.

The great men and women that inspire us have this buoyancy about them. They will not be distracted or moved off what they know the Holy Spirit is leading them in.

The Apostle Paul is, of course, one of these buoyant people. He experienced more bumps and hardships than most; yet he always rose above them.

Notice in 2 Corinthians 4:7-9, **But we have this treasure in earthen vessels, that the excellency of the power may be of God, and not us.**

**We are troubled on every side, yet not distressed; we are perplexed, but not in despair;**

**Persecuted, but not forsaken; cast down, but not destroyed.**

These statements were made by one who would not be intimidated! He had literally overcome every kind of attack by the power of God's treasure within him.

Many people quote these statements to identify Paul with their own misery. But if you are going to identify with his trouble, you must also identify with his buoyancy.

Read it again: . . . *not* distressed . . . *not* in despair . . . *not* forsaken . . . *not* destroyed. Look also at the ninth verse in the Phillips translation:

". . . we may be knocked down but we are never knocked out!" The greatest mistake you can make is to give up. When the issues of life come to squash you down, you must shake off the distress, the despair, and the discouragement that accompany them.

Cast off the feeling of being forsaken that Satan tries to amplify in your mind. Instead, encourage yourself with the words, **I will never leave thee, nor forsake thee** (Heb. 13:5). You are not forsaken! Stir up the forces of God's treasure within you and face the challenge with the power of God's Word.

There are times we must respond with a sense of spiritual violence. We must aggressively release the deposits of God that are stored up within. Jesus said, . . . **the kingdom of heaven suffereth violence, and the violent take it by force** (Matt. 11:12). You face your enemy or difficulty and you unleash the forces of God's awesome power.

The great prophet Elijah stood in the face of the prophets of the demonic god Baal. He alone challenged a total of 850 men and dared them to put their lives on the line, and to resolve the double standard Israel was living with. That day they would discover who was the true God, Baal or Jehovah.

With unshakable courage, Elijah mocked the false prophets as they attempted to conjure up a response from Baal. But there would be no response. When you trust in the wrong thing, you find yourself helpless in a time of true need.

Elijah prayed a simple and very powerful prayer, **Lord God of Abraham, Isaac, and of Israel, let it be known this day that thou art God in Israel, and that I am thy servant, and that I have done all these things at thy word** (1 Kings 18:36).

The result was dramatic. Jehovah God left no question of who the true God was. God will honor your courage just as He did Elijah's, when your courage comes from the same source.

Notice again Elijah's prayer. He said, ". . . let it be known . . . that I have done all these things at thy word." He was acting on what he had received specific direction to do. You will have God's favor activated regularly in your life only when you are sensitive to respond to His direct leading.

Joshua learned this the hard way. Soon after the triumph over Jericho, Joshua seemed unstoppable. The city of Ai was the next to be conquered, and the Israelites expected there would be little difficulty with this less powerful people. Joshua confidently sent a small army to take the city.

But the result was not as Joshua had anticipated. Thirty-six men were lost in the battle, a disturbing defeat. When Joshua came before the Lord, he discovered he had not gone out against Ai at the direction of the Holy Spirit. Instead, he had only presumed it was time to go. If he had gone first into the presence of God, he would have learned that there was sin that had to be dealt with before any more land would be conquered. Once he dealt with Achan's sin, then he could march on Ai with the power of God's Word going before them.

This man of courage was also a man quick to repent and quick to learn. From that time he never went into battle again without Jehovah God's Word, **Fear them not: for I have delivered them into thine hand** (Josh. 10:8). Israel never lost another man in battle, nor suffered another defeat.

David also learned this lesson of courage and restraint. In First Samuel chapter 30 David and his men returned to Ziklag from battle and found that the Amalekites had burned the city and taken their women and children. David did two very important things in response to this crisis.

First, he encouraged himself in the Lord his God, even though he was emotionally drained from the situation. In the same way, you must deliberately stir up the courage within you.

Proverbs 28:1 says, . . . **the righteous are bold as a lion.** The lion is fearless and violent, and will back down to no one. That same fearlessness must be stirred up within you.

When your enemy strikes, stir yourself by reaffirming your place in Christ. Speak out loud words that establish His love for you, and the power of His Word that is available to you. David activated courage in the Lord his God.

To *encourage* yourself is to activate courage. A resilience from within gives you the ability to emerge from, and many times, evade discouragement. You recover quickly. David activated his courage, but he knew there was more needed.

The second thing David did was to inquire of the Lord saying, **Shall I pursue after this troop? shall I overtake them?** (v. 8). Herein lies an important truth. Courage alone is not the total answer, even though it is courage in the Lord. There must be the clear direction from the Holy Spirit as well. When David was released by God to pursue his enemy, he went with utter confidence and he recovered everything just as God had said.

Courage is expressed in many different ways. Recently in one of our meetings I began to minister to husbands and fathers who needed to become the man of God in their homes. Several came to the front of the church to repent and receive strength to fulfill that responsibility. Some of them were prominent in the church. That took courage! That is facing a difficulty fearlessly. It is also being led by the heart and not by excuses.

When Elijah was faced with a situation that was less spectacular than dealing with the prophets of Baal, he found himself lacking. Instead of courageously confronting Jezebel's threats against him, he tucked his tail and didn't stop running the entire day.

Elijah was unable to be consistent. He was either in total command, or out of control; either extremely courageous, or very cowardly. What he lacked was temperance to regulate and direct his courage.

Jesus, our example, was of all men the most courageous; yet his entire life was marked by temperance. He didn't back down from any demon, nor from the religious hypocrites of His day. Later he courageously restrained Himself in the court of His accusers.

Many people have cultivated the habit of "speaking their minds" and "telling it like it is," and in doing so they cause a lot of hurt and damage to other people. They confuse their careless words for courage and thoughtlessness for honesty. Much of the time it takes greater courage to give a soft answer, or simply to say nothing at all. What we need are men and women of God who have developed a balanced blend of courage and temperance, who draw their strength from the indwelling Spirit.

The nature of Christ within a person should demonstrate a courage that is actively blended with temperance, and that will mix compassion with truth.

Armed with that type of stability, you will be able to approach the demands of life with the perspective of courage and strength, seasoned with temperance.

It was a lesson Joshua learned well and never forgot. After Ai he would not be defeated again. As long as you see with God's courage and strength, you need not be defeated either.

**Teach me thy way, O Lord, and lead me in a plain path, because of mine enemies.**

I had fainted, unless I had believed to see the goodness of the Lord in the land of the living.

Wait on the Lord: be of good courage, and he shall strengthen thine heart: wait, I say, on the Lord (Ps. 27:11,13,14).

# 7

# Victory Upon Victory

Joshua had come to understand God in a way that produced calm confidence. He had discovered that God's resources were available to him. He was convinced of the dependability of Jehovah God.

From his victory over Ai, Joshua was drawn into a battle against an alliance of five mountain kings. They had heard of the utter devastation of Ai. They reasoned that their only hope against the invasion of the Israeli army was to join their forces together. But regardless of their endeavors, they were powerless to stand against Israel.

Joshua did not hesitate in the face of his greatest challenge. To the surprise of his opponents, he marched through the night. He went in the assurance of God's Words, **Fear them**

**not: for I have delivered them into thine hand; there shall not a man of them stand before thee** (Josh. 10:8).

The challengers, suffering a great defeat, turned and began to flee. But God's Word had declared total victory for Israel, therefore God rose up to fight for them. He sent a great storm and hailstones to destroy the enemies.

The inspiration of this divine intervention brought Joshua into a new dimension of faith in God. Joshua spoke directly to the sun and moon to stand still in the heavens. This additional daylight gave Israel the time they needed to bring a resounding victory over their enemy. Notice God responded to the word of a man and the sun and moon stood still.

Joshua was in complete cooperation and partnership with Jehovah God. Because of that relationship, God moved to stop the rotation of the earth and yet continue the normal forces of gravity and pressure. It was a day unparalleled in human history.

The kings fled to a cave to hide themselves, but Joshua ordered it sealed with huge stones and had men set on guard lest the kings escape. Once the conquered cities were secured, Joshua returned to the cave. He brought the kings out to face the commanders of the Israeli armies, who put their feet on the necks of the kings. This symbolized Israel's total victory. It also brought into clear focus God's covenant with His nation — that they would possess every place upon which the soles of their feet would tread.

With this huge military triumph came a great sense of power and influence with God. But, rather than standing back in contentment, Joshua continued to press on to victory upon victory. City after city and king after king would be consumed by this powerful and irresistible force. Before Joshua rested, thirty-one kings and kingdoms would fall. Israel had an assurance of faith in their God that could not be quenched. They would make known the presence and power of Jehovah God to every intruder in God's land.

Once you, as a believer, begin to recognize and affirm in your own life this conquering attitude the Holy Spirit has over your enemy, you will be lifted into enormous confidence. You can see clearly in Psalm 18:39,40 how He wants to put *your* foot on *your* enemy's neck.

**For thou hast girded me with strength unto the battle: thou hast subdued under me those that rose up against me.**

**Thou hast also given me the necks of mine enemies; that I might destroy them that hate me.**

Of course, our enemy is not people but the principalities and powers in heavenly places. God has infused us with His strength and might to see through the *symptoms* of the problem and discover the *source*.

God has broken the cycle of reproach, discouragement, and failure. If you will embrace His attitude, a momentum of triumph will begin to build from the depth of your being. You will acquire an unshakable grip on His strength in your inner man. You will not be intimidated by the tactics of the adversary.

Philippians 1:28 in *The Amplified Bible* says it best. "And do not [for a moment] be frightened or intimidated in anything by your opponents and adversaries, for such [constancy and fearlessness] will be a clear sign (proof and seal) to them of [their impending] destruction; but [a sure token and evidence] of your deliverance and salvation, and that from God."

In a meeting I was conducting, a lovely lady came for prayer and this scripture became very clear. She had been ministered to deeply by the Holy Spirit. The very next morning she received the results of an earlier medical test. The test showed a definite cancerous mass in one breast.

As she stood before me this scripture from Philippians rose up from deep in my spirit. As I spoke the words she could feel their power penetrating her body. Later, she went back for more tests, and to the amazement of the examiners the cancerous mass had completely disappeared. No type of mass was found whatsoever!

One of our enemy's most devastating tactics is fear and intimidation. If he can draw you into his arena, he will begin to control you with confusion and a sense of uncertainty. But when the reality of Jesus' victory comes alive inside, you can gain success in any struggle or endeavor.

Joshua's victory went far beyond his own ability. He continued to march on with increased assurance. His successes would not come through human effort alone. He had become thoroughly convinced that he was not limited to his own strength; instead, he had access to God's limitless power.

There were three underlying principles that brought Joshua from one victory to another. These simple principles can be keys for your own continued spiritual advancement.

The first was a heart of diligent commitment to do all that God had commanded. He read before all of Israel the commandments which Moses had been given. Joshua 11:23 says he did all that the Lord had said to Moses. He left nothing undone.

It is vitally important that we do not become slack in our pursuit of God's lifestyle and direction. We must become diligent to take to heart the importance of God's dealing and direction in our lives.

God gave the promise because He expects us to live in it. If we can approach God with the same heart of commitment Joshua displayed, we can be led into the promises He has set before us.

Don't be slack, but determine to fulfill all that God has spoken. Determine to live committed without compromise. To "commit" yourself means simply to deliver yourself into another's charge. God's direction should have complete authority in the decisions you make.

Joshua learned to move into battle under the direct leadership of the Holy Spirit. The plans and strategies were not his own, but came through communion with God. Your diligence to allow God to direct the details of your life will prove to be an important key to obtaining what has seemed unobtainable.

The second principle Joshua revealed was boldness to occupy new territory. We cannot allow the successes we have seen in the past to delude us into thinking that we have come far enough. We must not yield to spiritual stagnation. Stagnant water may be peaceful but it becomes a breeding ground for very unpleasant growth.

Joshua went from victory to victory, and we are told to go from glory to glory. Second Corinthians 3:18 from *The Amplified Bible* gives powerful insight on taking new territory in our life. "And all of us, as with unveiled face, [because we] continued to behold [in the Word of God] as in a mirror the glory of the Lord, are constantly being transfigured into His very own image in ever increasing splendor and from one degree of glory to another; [for this comes] from the Lord [Who is] the Spirit."

Your diligence before God to allow His Words to be absorbed into your being brings continual change. We pass from one degree of glory to another, as one said it, until we reach our Master's degree.

The question that Joshua asked Israel rings out to us today: **How long are ye slack to go to possess the Land, which the Lord God of your fathers hath given you?** (Josh. 18:3). We must set aside stagnation and reach out to obtain fresh water and new territory.

The third principle for pursuing victory upon victory is a deep confidence in God's faithfulness to His promise. In Joshua 21:45 from the

Berkeley version, notice what is written: "Of all the good promises which the Lord had made to the house of Israel, not one failed; they were all fulfilled."

Again from the Berkeley version in 2 Corinthians 1:20, "In Him all the promises of God are yes. For this reason we also say through Him 'Amen' to God for His glory through us."

When God gives a promise He also gives the power to cause it to come to pass. When we simply add our agreement with it, we obtain the power of God for that promise. God cannot be changed from being a faithful God. His Words are as sure as the dawn (see Hos. 6:3). There is a sustaining power deep within that continues to remind us that God will fulfill every promise He has made.

He remained faithful through all of Israel's rebellious wanderings in the wilderness. As they stepped into a steady walk of loyalty to God, they activated the power within the promise. His faithfulness to them became apparent as they faced each obstacle. They were filled with such enormous confidence and unflinching faith that no enemy could stand successfully against them.

God responded again and again to their faith. Notice Joshua 21:43,44, again from the Berkeley version, "The Lord gave Israel the whole land which He promised their fathers to give them. They took possession of it and lived in it. The Lord gave them peace on every side, according to all that He had promised their ancestors. None of their enemies could withstand them, because the Lord delivered all their enemies into their hands."

They were in the land of their dreams. Living in peace! All their enemies had been conquered. GOD HAD REMAINED FAITHFUL!!

That is the God we serve. He has defeated every enemy that challenges you. He is faithful to you, and will make every promise a reality in your life. You can possess the land of your dreams and begin to live in them.

There is today an immense need for God's holy nation of believers to embrace this same unshakable confidence in God's faithfulness. Let God show His faithfulness to you.

Israel was entering the days of victory and tranquility. The people spent several years moving into the land they were to inherit. Not only had God liberated them from Egypt and their wanderings, but now there was liberty from the constant warfare in Canaan.

Along with victory and liberty in Christ comes a new challenge to spiritual stability. There is a tendency to drop our guard to Satan's more subtle attacks. It demands as much spiritual diligence to maintain a position as it does to obtain it. Times of peace can be deceptive. Though the conflict on the outside may have ceased, pressures can arise from within that are just as deadly.

Many who have stood through great trouble and conquered, later found themselves defeated because of sloppy spiritual conduct in times of seeming peace. Our confidence can never rest in the accomplishments or achievements of the past, but only in our continual place in the presence of God.

Through maintaining a deep and intimate communion with God we have the assurance of victory upon victory. You have the Spirit of God to overcome any obstacle or challenge. The same spiritual principles that clearly brought Joshua into the inheritance of his dreams have never altered; they will keep you on course as well.

# 8

# Vision To Possess
# Your Dreams

Joshua had achieved what had seemed impossible. He had brought this nation to a place of utter dedication and total victory in the land of Canaan. One man's fearless faith had lifted an entire nation from oppression and poverty into power and prosperity in the presence of God.

Israel was in possession of the land of their dreams. All their lives, they had heard how their father Abraham had come into this place of promise in obedience to God. Now they stood, not merely in the memory of Abraham's past greatness, but in the reality of God's greatness that had been revealed to them.

Joshua was very old. He had rallied the nation not to himself, but to

God. His entire life had demonstrated the potential of one who is single-minded in his devotion to God. As he addressed the elders for the last time, he pointed them only to God. There was a marked absence of any self-exaltation or recitation of his own achievements. He reminded them of the past mercy and faithfulness of Jehovah. He urged them to continue in the power of their relationship with God and unwavering loyalty to Him.

Then, like the leader he had always been, he clearly affirmed his own unbending position: **. . . as for me and my house, we will serve the Lord** (Josh. 24:15).

With that statement, Joshua summed up all that he knew and felt. His life would end in the same victory and devotion that he had consistently embraced. He would point them to God alone.

The success of his leadership was proved when the response of the elders rang out. **And the Lord drave out from**

**before us all the people, even the Amorites which dwelt in the land: therefore will we also serve the Lord; for he is our God** (v. 18).

Joshua was a man of vision. He led Israel into victory and filled them with his vision. He gave them the ability to see beyond what faced them and to become totally aware of the greatness of their God. God trained him to look beyond the immediate to the ultimate result.

To have vision means exactly that: "to see beyond ordinary sight, to perceive a revelation or glimpse beyond the natural world."

God gave Israel a vision that would transport them out of their immediate situation and into His plan. When Joshua would run with the vision, Israel would follow.

Proverbs 29:18 says, **Where there is no vision, the people perish.** In this scripture, vision takes on two vital aspects.

First, it is vision of our redemption. Joshua instilled within God's people the confidence that He would fight for them. He would be their deliverer from every enemy. They were God's nation of conquerors.

Likewise, you and I must see the redemption that Jesus bought for mankind. He has made us sons of the Living God! He has given us a position with God and dominion over the power of darkness!

You can look beyond the temporal to the eternal. Beyond your weaknesses to His strength. Beyond sickness to His health. Beyond lack and into His abundance.

With a vision of Christ's victory, you take on victory. The Conybeare translation of 2 Corinthians 2:14 brings great enlightenment: "But thanks be to God who leads me on from place to place in the train of his triumph, to celebrate his victory over the enemies of Christ; and by me sends forth the knowledge of Him, a steam of fragrant incense, throughout the world."

As your vision of redemption increases, so does your victory, just as Israel's confidence increased as Jehovah's revelations unfolded.

Second, it is a vision of direction. Israel wandered aimlessly for forty years, unconvinced of God's direction. The people lived from day to day without understanding the purpose for their lives. Having no vision, they became subject to discontent. Without vision, we too can wander in uncertainty. When a person has no vision for the direction in which God is leading, it is easy to slip into discouragement.

In fact, to "perish" in this verse means to loosen, become lawless and undisciplined. Where there is no vision, dream, or pursuit of God's plan, people become loose, undisciplined, and discouraged.

Israel began to see that when they remained close to God, the land of their dreams came within their grasp.

When you begin to perceive the vision that God places before you, a hunger and desire to remain close to God will emerge. Your desire will be to walk in the dream within your heart. By remaining pliable and open to God's influence, you will see His direction in detail. Then the hope that His plan brings will keep you from becoming discouraged.

The vision of the new land of God's promise kept Joshua alive. He would not rest until he conquered all and dwelt within that vision. It provided the direction for his life.

In the same way, God wants His direction in your life. It may be a vision to spend more time with God in prayer. It could be a vision for your business, your home, or your ministry.

People who do not have God's vision are not bothered by their lack of discipline. They have no dream. But those who through Jesus Christ have obtained insight into the mysteries of life choose to walk under the guidance of God's influence. They are the people who will not fail to fulfill any of God's plans.

The book of Hebrews, chapter 6, tells us that Jesus was our forerunner into the presence and promise of God. Jesus stands today as our High Priest in heaven that He might give to us a vision of our redemption and direction. Jesus sent the Spirit of heaven into the earth to plant in you all of the greatness God had for mankind. Jesus went before us and unlocked all of the mysteries of life. The seeds of heaven are deposited within you to possess and retain His vision.

Second Peter 1:3,4 says, **According as his divine power hath given unto us all things that pertain unto life and godliness, through the knowledge of him that hath called us to glory and virtue:**

**Whereby are given unto us exceeding great and precious promises: that by these ye might be partakers of the divine nature, having**

**escaped the corruption that is in the world through lust.**

He has given us divine — godlike — power and ability to deal with anything we face in life. We participate and share the godlike nature by absorbing and acting on the visions of revelation and direction. Jesus obtained them first on our behalf, and as we follow in His footsteps, led by the Spirit of heaven, we will possess and retain all things.

We not only possess land, but we also possess complete liberation: spirit, soul and body. Notice in James 4:7, **Submit yourselves therefore to God. Resist the devil, and he will flee from you.**

Through simple submission to God — to His vision, His revelation, His direction — you align yourself with Him. His power becomes effective within you. Now when you resist your enemy, God too will stand and fight for you.

The Wuest translation puts it this way, "Stand immovable against the onset of the devil and he will flee from you."

Satan will come to take back from you whatever ground you have gained. He won't come just once or twice, but hundreds of times and in a variety of ways.

Joshua was fully aware that their enemies would try to regain the land. Israel would be responsible for keeping the inheritance they had obtained. Joshua imparted to the people the same qualities that had made him great with God. They declared to Joshua, **The Lord our God will we serve, and his voice will we obey** (Josh. 24:24). That is quite different from what Moses had heard. Now they accepted the responsibility to maintain their position through serving Jehovah.

Joshua gave this nation vision. He had given them vision to move from aimless wandering to conquering. He had infused them with the vision to dominate the land of their dreams under the guidance of the Almighty God.

In this time of farewell, he once again kindled the fire of their vision to continue living out the dream. They had finally come to a land of rest. The rest that they obtained was never to be fully completed, but it pointed ahead to Christ.

Joshua's life had been a life of leadership and a life of service. He had served God faithfully. His service to God was complete, for he had brought God's nation into the experience of the promise.

In his death, as in life, he was crowned with the dignity and honor by being called "the servant of the Lord."

In all you do in life, richness and fulfillment comes when you seek to remain a servant of the Lord.

# 9

# Principles of War

Great victories come out of great conflict. The very thought of winning implies a contest or battle. In Christian living we are not naive about the dangers we face. We know that our commitment to pursue God's great promise puts us on the list for satanic attention.

There is a spiritual conflict which persists against God's holy nation today — the Body of Christ. This conflict exists because it is through His people that God plans to reveal His wisdom to the principalities and powers in the heavenlies.

The victory Jesus gained over death has forever sealed your freedom to dominate and conquer any attack against you. He has placed in your grasp all the tools and weapons sufficient to defeat the enemy.

Our battles are waged in the realm of the spirit. Our greatest triumphs are hidden from public view. But they are known in the spirit.

The principles of war against Satan's strategies are vital to continually control his aggression. The great leaders in the Bible who successfully moved God's people through difficult times had a firm grip on the promise of God and the principles that would cause them to conquer.

They had faith to stand and confidence to continue, regardless of the opposition. That spirit of victory and confidence must stir in you as well.

You must recover and maintain your confidence in your ability to wield power effectively. You cannot cower in fear but instead you must stand tall with unwavering faith.

Jesus' sacrifice for mankind puts all people who will yield to Him in position to defeat all the plans Satan brings against them.

In 1 John 3:8 the Word says, **For this purpose the Son of God was manifested, that he might destroy the works of the devil.**

Through His death Jesus has loosened and dissolved Satan's grip on mankind. God's new nation of redeemed people is rising up and taking charge. They are no longer under the control of the wicked one, but they have become masters over sin and Satan. That was the purpose of Jesus' coming: to make you a master and no longer a slave.

The battle and spiritual struggle for control in your life is waged in the arena of your soul. Notice in 1 Peter 2:11, **Dearly beloved, I beseech you as strangers and pilgrims, abstain from fleshly lusts, which war against the soul.** The strength of Satan's kingdom is sin. Through temptation and strong desires of your flesh he wars against your mind. If he can control the direction of your thoughts, he can prevent you from yielding to the flow of the Holy Spirit.

One of his spiritual warfare strategies is to absorb your energy. Satan can successfully stop a believer's progress by simply redirecting the focus of his attention.

Your focus determines the direction and level of your faith and energy. Jesus said, "The lamp of the body is the eye. When your eye is in single focus, sound, and fulfilling its function, also your whole body is well lighted" (Luke 11:34 Wuest).

Those distractions come in a variety of forms. They can be friends, issues, family, or other Christians. Even questions over Bible doctrines can become a distraction from the true purpose of God's work.

But when your eye is focused on God's promise and plan, it will fill you with the direction and strength of His light. In the martial arts, an idea is taught that helps illustrate this point.

When a trained expert stands in front of a stack of bricks he intends to break, he does not focus his attention and energy on the object itself. He focuses beyond it. One friend who holds the black belt rank says that when he faces a stack of bricks he focuses on going through the floor. The reason is that the point of your focus is where your energy ends. In the same way, when you direct your attention and the center of your interest on the promise and plan of God, it will carry you through any obstacle until you fully reach the point of your focus.

This is why we must continually reexamine the point of our focus. If I am no longer focusing on God's main issues in my life, I can find that the light I once walked in is growing dim.

Jesus went on to say in Luke 11:35, "Be constantly scrutinizing yourself therefore lest the light which is in you is darkness" (Wuest).

Your faith and energy can be absorbed when your focus is turned from power strengtheners to power stealers. Once a man had an opportunity to ask a lion trainer a question he had held for many years. As a boy going to the circus he had watched the trainers in the great cage with the dangerous cats. He wondered about the tools the man carried into the cage. He had a whip in his hand, a gun on his belt, and a four legged stool.

It was easy to understand the whip and the gun. A cat who made the wrong move would pay a price. But what about the stool?

The trainer explained that the stool was his most important tool. When he put that stool in front of a big cat, it tried to focus on all four legs of the stool at the same time. As long as the cat's attention was so divided, the trainer knew it could not make any sudden moves.

Disappointments can become distractions. The shortcomings or failure of others or even yourself can so pull your attention that you stumble.

Then the Mighty One who dwells within takes second place. As long as your enemy can keep you distracted from the real source of your strength, he will keep you powerless, paralyzed, and predictable. He need not worry about you. You will remain mesmerized by the strength stealers.

In 2 Chronicles 32, this strategy of Satan is graphically displayed. Sennacherib, king of Assyria, had come to capture Jerusalem and its king, Hezekiah.

God's Word was in Hezekiah's mouth when he told them **Be strong and courageous, be not afraid nor dismayed for the king of Assyria, nor for all the multitude that is with him: for there be more with us than with him.**

**With him is an arm of flesh; but with us is the Lord our God to help us, and to fight our battles. And the people rested themselves upon the words of Hezekiah king of Judah** (vv. 7,8).

111

The threat against God's people was very serious. They had been at peace. Now everything was in jeopardy.

Hezekiah pointed the people toward their strength and confidence. God was with them and He would fight their battles.

Sennacherib sent his messengers to challenge their faith in Jehovah God.

**Know ye not what I and my fathers have done unto all the people of other lands? Were the gods of the nations of those lands any ways able to deliver their lands out of mine hand? Now therefore let not Hezekiah deceive you, nor persuade you on this manner, neither yet believe him: for no god of any nation or kingdom was able to deliver his people out of mine hand, and out of the hand of my fathers: how much less shall your God deliver you out of mine hand?** (vv. 13,15)

It all sounded so impossible. Judah's enemy had built a very strong case. No one had escaped the grasp of Sennacherib's armies.

But the people held to the words of comfort which Hezekiah had given them. Then he and the prophet Isaiah prayed and cried out to God. Through their faith and prayer to God there was released an angel of the Lord, which went to fight their battle. By the next morning, the mighty men of the Assyrian army had been cut off and their plans crippled.

Spiritual warfare means holding tirelessly to the power of Christ's finished work and from that position of strong confidence remaining steadfast against any attack until victory is won.

In time, you begin to recognize the plans of your enemy as he tries to threaten you. The Holy Spirit within will spring up with a sharp resistance against the unseen spiritual forces.

The natural man is no match for Satan and demon powers. You will not successfully stand against his attacks with natural human effort and willpower. As long as you remain in natural thinking, you take a place below the powers of darkness.

Mastery over the kingdom of darkness depends upon your seeing from God's viewpoint, thinking His thoughts, and knowing His ways and plans. Notice James 1:22-25: "But prove yourselves doers of the word, and not merely hearers who delude themselves.

"For if anyone is a hearer of the word and not a doer, he is like a man who looks at his natural face in a mirror;

"for once he has looked at himself and gone away, he has immediately forgotten what kind of person he was.

"But one who looks intently at the perfect law, the law of liberty, and abides by it, not having become a forgetful hearer but an effectual doer, this man shall be blessed in what he does" (NAS).

When you look into God's Word, you find a picture of the new creation in Christ. You see the plan for total domination over every aspect of Satan's domain. You find the weapons that can cause you to stand strong.

Those who retain a firm grasp of the image they see of themselves in Christ establish the law of God's liberty in their own lives. They continue as Paul directed in Hebrews 12:2 and 3, **Looking unto Jesus the author and finisher of our faith . . . lest ye be wearied and faint in your minds.** *The Amplified Bible* reads, "Looking away [from all that will distract] to Jesus." To continue in God's laws, which create liberty, is to remain focused on Jesus and look away from the cares and distractions of this world.

Those who hear but do not embrace God's law for victory forget the power and presence of God that is available for their problems. They resort to human effort to face their battles. You cannot remain confident in something you have forgotten. Psalm 78:9-11 says, "The sons of Ephraim were archers equipped with bows, Yet they turned back in the day of battle. They did not keep the covenant of God, and refused to walk in His law; And they forgot his deeds, And His miracles that He had shown them" (NAS).

When they faced the battle, though they had the weapons, they turned back. They forgot the greatness of God. They saw only the greatness of their enemy. In Exodus 13, verse 17, God would not leave His people near the land of the Philistines, **Lest peradventure the people repent when they see war, and they return to Egypt.**

Many today prefer to remain in captivity rather than face the demands of battle. People are losing to someone who is already defeated. Satan was crushed in Christ's victory. Our enemy cannot defeat us; he can only make us quit.

When you come to the end of your strength, and you are on the threshold of fainting, you can stir up the deposit of God within you. **He giveth power to the faint; and to them that have no might he increaseth strength. Even the youths shall faint and be weary, and the young men shall utterly fall: But they that wait upon the Lord shall renew their strength; they shall mount up with wings as eagles; they shall run, and not be weary; and they shall walk, and not faint.** (Is. 40:29-31).

Strength will increase as you wait on Him. To wait does not mean to remain passive until He moves. It means to build yourself together with Him, joining yourself closely to Him in a confident and expectant way. As you do, your strength is renewed.

The actual implication is that you will exchange your weakness for His strength. Now in Him you stand strong in the day Satan challenges you. You are solidly founded in the Lord. Fearlessly, you draw upon the resources of heaven, confident that in the authority of Jesus' name you can command every attack of darkness to flee from you.

Your life of seeking to walk close to God can keep you sensitive to the Spirit as you deal with satanic attacks.

James 4:7 says, "Be subject with implicit obedience to God at once and once for all. Stand immovable against the onset of the devil and he will flee from you" (Wuest).

First set your face toward God, fill yourselves with His Word and His presence. Then refuse to move toward any desire, thought, or action which would be unwelcome in His presence. Satan's pressure cannot prevail against that solid stand. Instead, he will flee from you.

The strong defense of your current position is vital, but it is not the total picture. You have been created for advancement. You have a desire for increase. God never intended for you to hold your position without taking new ground. He has placed within you the spirit of a conqueror.

The cry deep within is that your union with Christ will draw you deeper in Him. The Word of God within you hungers for victory and advancement. It takes an offensive to advance. Notice Romans 12:21 from the Phillips. "Don't allow yourself to be overpowered by evil. Take the offensive — overcome evil with good!"

You don't need to live under pressure. You can begin to apply the pressure. God's kingdom of light removes darkness.

There are some key points important to our advancement.

First, pinpoint the objective! The objective is the target area. You must discern the goal which God is setting before you. What is the single most important area which He would have you concentrate on? He may set before you something which seems unobtainable. He specializes in leading people to obtain the unobtainable. He turns setbacks into successes, troubles into triumphs. Let Him focus you on His victory.

Second, take the offensive. You will notice in Ephesians 6, verse 11, as the Apostle Paul directs us to "put on the whole armour of God" an important detail. There are three things to *have* done, and three things to do for victory. You *have* strengthened your mind with truth. You *have* put on the breastplate of righteousness. You *have* shod your feet.

You stand in a strong position. Now you must do something.

You must *take* the shield of faith, You must *take* the helmet of salvation to protect your thoughts. You must *take* the sword of the Spirit to cut through every stronghold. You move forward to *take* the weapons of spiritual victory.

Third, you must occupy the land. There can be no hesitation. Once you have defeated your enemy and opened new doors in your life, take total possession of this new territory.

Finally, you must maintain security. Israel's history demonstrates the consequence of failing to continue in the same strength and trust in God. The land they once possessed they later lost and would struggle to regain.

Proverbs 4:23 says, **Keep thy heart with all diligence; for out of it are the issues of life.**

God makes deposits which he expects you to maintain. Never lose ground. Keep a firm grip on what you have possessed and continue to build. Paul summed up this point in 2 Timothy 2:3-6. "Put up with your share of hardship as a loyal soldier in Christ's army. Remember: 1. That no soldier on active service gets himself entangled in business, or he will not please his commanding officer. 2. A man who enters an athletic contest wins no prize unless he keeps the rules laid down. 3. Only the man who works on the land has the right to the first share of its produce" (Phillips).

Our service is to Jesus. We live for Him and our loyalty must not be divided. The fruit of a life devoted to Him is that we can live in places He has planned for us and possess the promises far beyond provisions.

God's door of deliverance is open to you. He will be your strength and shield. He will fight your battles. In Him you can conquer life's conflicts.

# References

*The Amplified Bible, New Testament.* Copyright © 1954, 1958 by The Lockman Foundation, La Habra, California.

*The Amplified Bible, Old Testament.* Copyright © 1962, 1964 by Zondervan Publishing House, Grand Rapids, Michigan.

*The Life and Epistles of St. Paul.* Reprinted 1980 by W. J. Conybeare and J. S. Howson. Wm. B. Eerdmans Publishing Company, Grand Rapids, Michigan.

*The Living Bible* (TLB). Copyright © 1971, by Tyndale House Publishers, Wheaton, Illinois.

*The Modern Language Bible, The New Berkeley Version in Modern English.* Copyright © 1945, 1959, 1969 by Zondervan Publishing House, Grand Rapids, Michigan.

# Books by Dennis Burke

*Knowing God Intimately*

*Diligence*
*A Guide to Successfully Attaining*
*Your God-Given Goals*

*How To Meditate God's Word*

*Visitation of the Holy Spirit*

*Understanding the Fear of the Lord*

**Available from your local bookstore
or from:**

HARRISON HOUSE
P. O. Box 35035
Tulsa, OK 74153

For a complete list of tapes and books by Dennis Burke or to receive his publication, *Words to the Wise*, write:

Dennis Burke Ministries
P. O. Box 150043
Arlington, TX 76015

*Please include your prayer
requests and comments
when you write.*